CAMBRIDGE
Alphabet Book

Olga Gasparova

CAMBRIDGE
UNIVERSITY PRESS

1 Write.

2 Write letter **a**.

 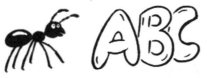   

__pple   __nt   __lph__bet   __eropl__ne   __rm   b__n__n__

3 Write.

4 Write letter **b**.

__us   __ike   __ed   __all   __read   __ee

5 Circle the odd one out.

a a a a a a a a e a a a a a a a   b b b b b b b b b b d b b b b

2

1 Write.

C C ⌐ᶜ

c c ⌐ᶜ

2 Write letter **c**.

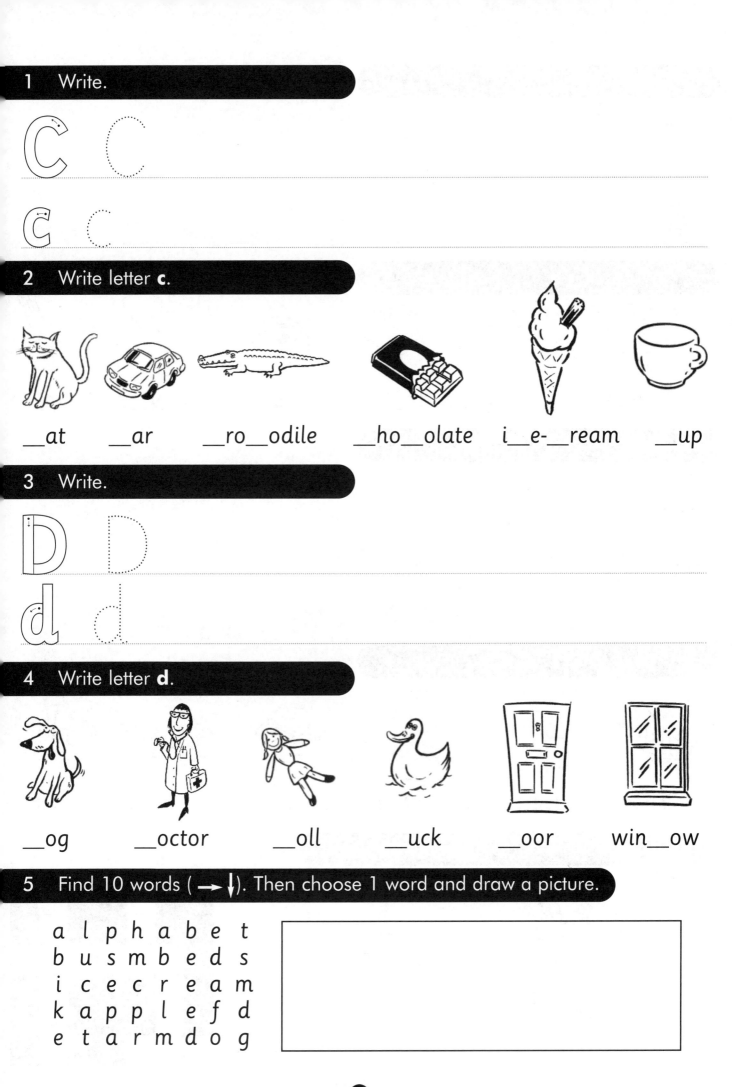

__at   __ar   __ro__odile   __ho__olate   i__e-__ream   __up

3 Write.

D D

d d

4 Write letter **d**.

__og   __octor   __oll   __uck   __oor   win__ow

5 Find 10 words (⟶↓). Then choose 1 word and draw a picture.

```
a l p h a b e t
b u s m b e d s
i c e c r e a m
k a p p l e f d
e t a r m d o g
```

1 Write.

E E

e e

2 Write letter e.

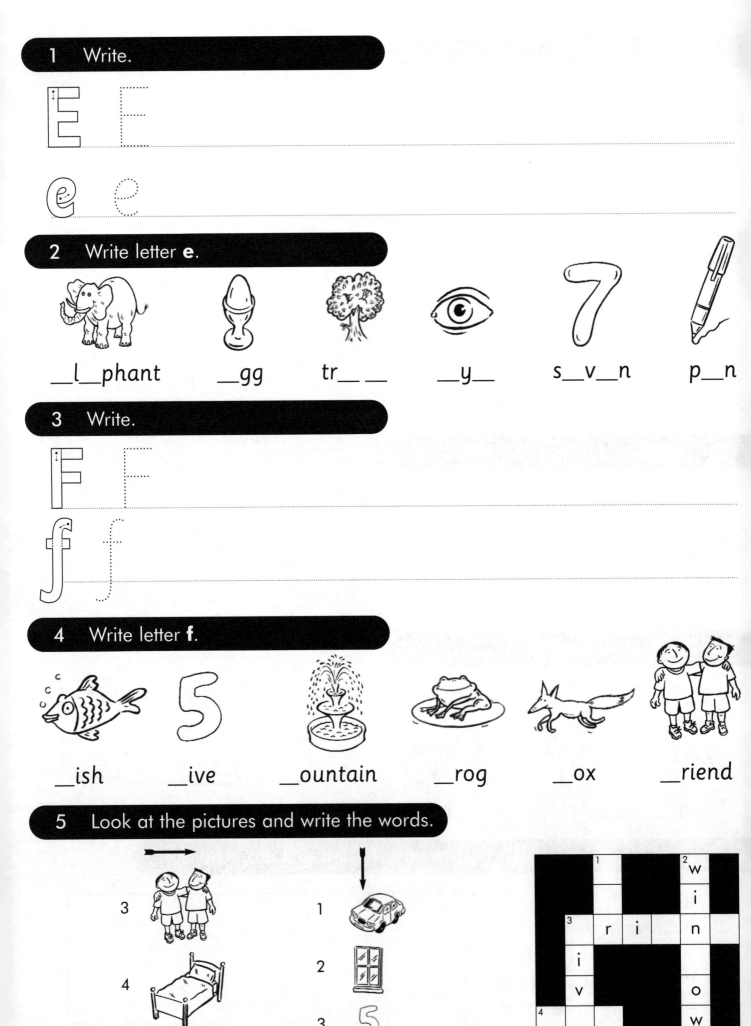

__l__phant   __gg   tr__ __   __y__   s__v__n   p__n

3 Write.

F F

f f

4 Write letter f.

__ish   __ive   __ountain   __rog   __ox   __riend

5 Look at the pictures and write the words.

3

4

1

2

3

		¹			²w
					i
³	r	i		n
	i			
	v			o
⁴				w

4

1 Write.

G G

g g

2 Write letter **g**.

_uitar   _irl   _oose   kan_aroo   le_   fla_

3 Write.

H H

h h

4 Write letter **h**.

_and   _orse   _at   _ouse   eig_t   c_air

5 Write small and capital letters.

B → ☐   H → ☐   ☐ ← e

☐ ← g   ☐ ← c   ☐ ← a

F → ☐   D → ☐

1 Write.

I I

i i

2 Write letter **i**.

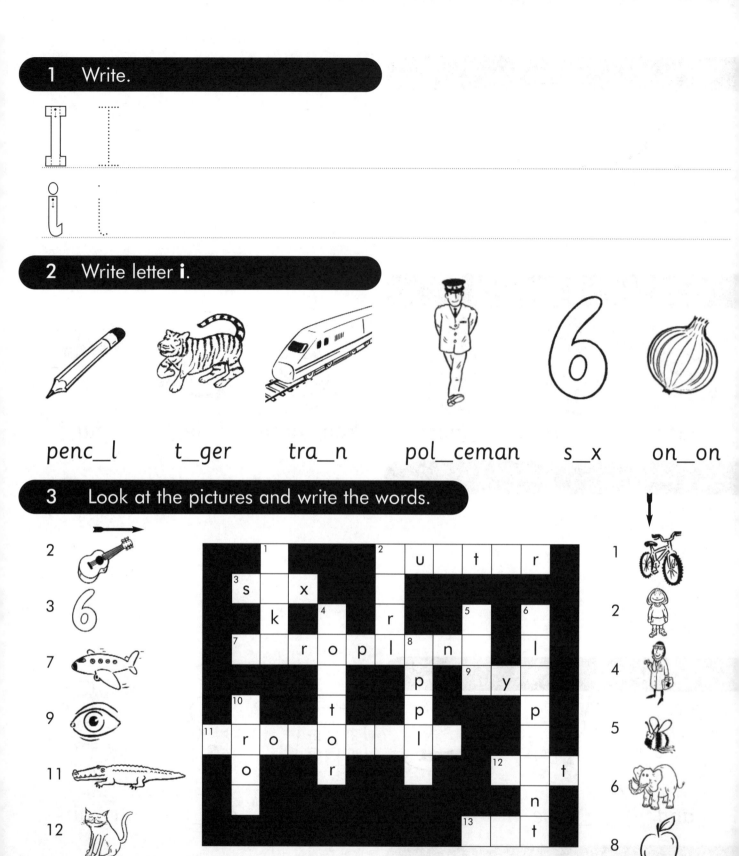

penc_l   t_ger   tra_n   pol_ceman   s_x   on_on

3 Look at the pictures and write the words.

4 Find 6 words and write them.

eabdogfeggafishacbeedflaglicbedfg

1 Write.

J J

j j

2 Write letter **j**.

_eans _uice _am _ump _acket _umper

3 Write.

K K

k k

4 Write letter **k**.

_ing _ey _ite boo_ duc_ soc_s

5 Match and colour.

K   B   a   c

E   F   g   f

J   D   A   i   j   h

I   H   d   b

C   G   e   k

7

1 Write.

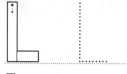

2 Write letter **l**.

   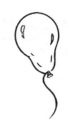 

_emon   __o_ __ipop   _eopard   ba_ _oon   fami_y

3 Write.

4 Write letter **m**.

__ilk   __oon   __an   __ouse   co_puter   u_brella

5 Find 10 words (→↓). Write the words.

n	b	d	l	l	f	o	x
c	o	m	p	u	t	e	r
a	o	h	c	t	r	m	s
r	k	i	n	g	e	a	i
m	i	l	k	p	e	n	x

→

_ ox

_ o _ put_r

_ _ n _

_ _ _ _ _

p_n

↓

_ _ r

_ oo _

tr_ _

_ _ n

s_x

8

1 Write.

N N N

n n n

2 Write letter **n**.

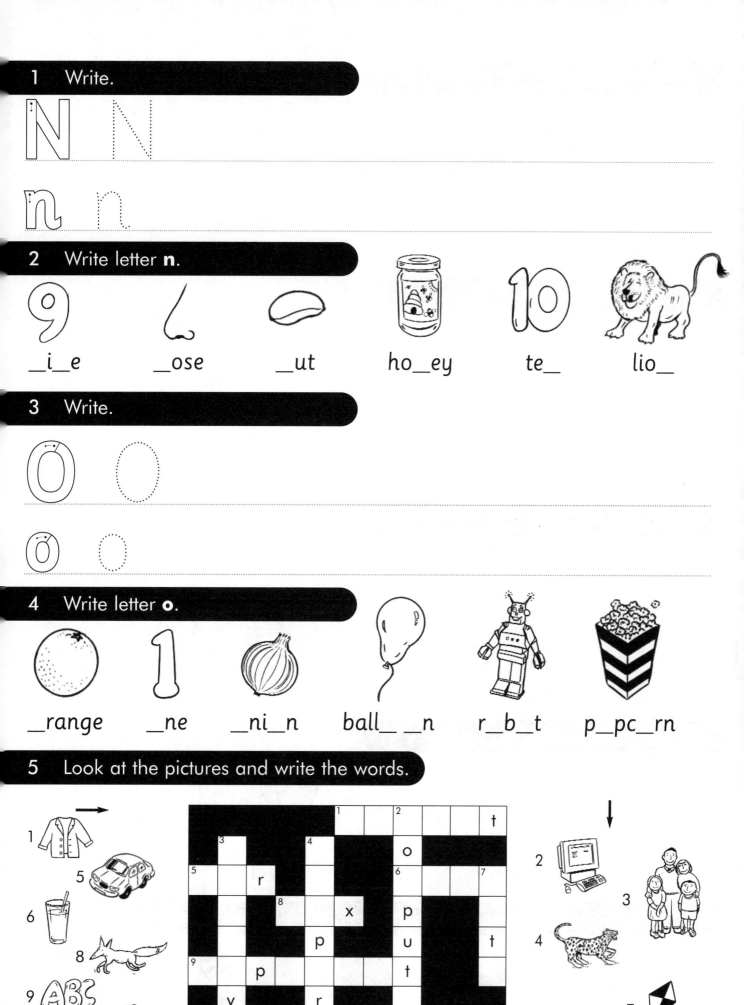

_i_e   _ose   _ut   ho_ey   te_   lio_

3 Write.

O O

O O

4 Write letter **o**.

_range   _ne   _ni_n   ball_ _n   r_b_t   p_pc_rn

5 Look at the pictures and write the words.

1 Write.

P P
p p

2 Write letter p.

_arrot   _icture   _oliceman   a_ _le   _en

3 Write.

Q Q
q q

4 Write letter q.

_ueen   _uestion   _uick   s_uirrel   s_uare   _uiet

5 What is this? Write the words and colour the pictures.

1 Look at the pictures and write the words.

→

3

4

7

10

11

12

↓

1

2

4

5

6

8

9

11

2 Write.

R R

r r

3 Write letter **r**.

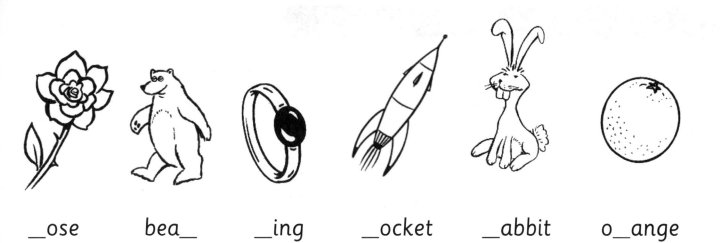

ose   bea   _ing   _ocket   _abbit   o_ange

1 Write.

S S

S s

2 Write letter **s**.

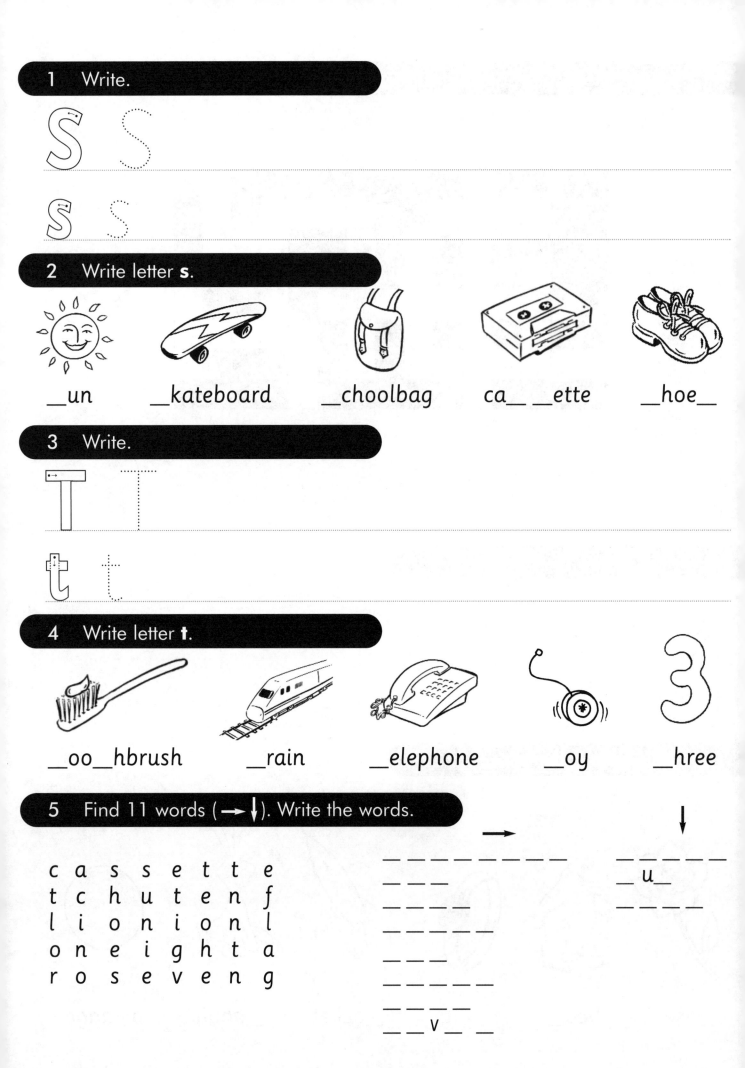

__un   __kateboard   __choolbag   ca__ __ette   __hoe__

3 Write.

T

t

4 Write letter **t**.

__oo__hbrush   __rain   __elephone   __oy   __hree

5 Find 11 words (→↓). Write the words.

c	a	s	s	e	t	t	e
t	c	h	u	t	e	n	f
l	i	o	n	i	o	n	l
o	n	e	i	g	h	t	a
r	o	s	e	v	e	n	g

→

_ _ _ _ _ _ _ _
_ _ _
_ _ _ _
_ _ _ _ _
_ _ _
_ _ _ _ _
_ _ _ _
_ _ v _ _

↓

_ _ _ _ _
_ u _
_ _ _ _

12

1 Write.

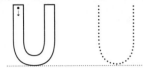

2 Write letter u.

__mbrella

j__mp

fo__r

c__p

j__ice

r__n

3 Look at the pictures and write the words.

3

6

9

11

12

13

14

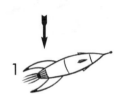

1

2

4

5

7

8

10

1 Write.

V V

V v

2 Write letter **v**.

__ideo   se__en   ri__er   __ase   en__elope

3 Write.

W W

W w

4 Write letter **w**.

__indo__   __itch   __atch   t__o   __ater   co__

5 Find 10 words (→↓). Write the words.

→   ↓

w	d	x	t	h	r	e	e
q	u	e	s	t	i	o	n
c	c	w	f	i	v	e	u
a	k	v	i	d	e	o	t
t	i	g	e	r	r	u	n

_ _ _ _ _   _ _ _

_ _ _ _ _ _ _ _   _ _ _

_ _ _ _   _ _ _ _

_ _ _ _ _

_ _ _

1 Write.

X X X

X X X

2 Write letter **x**.

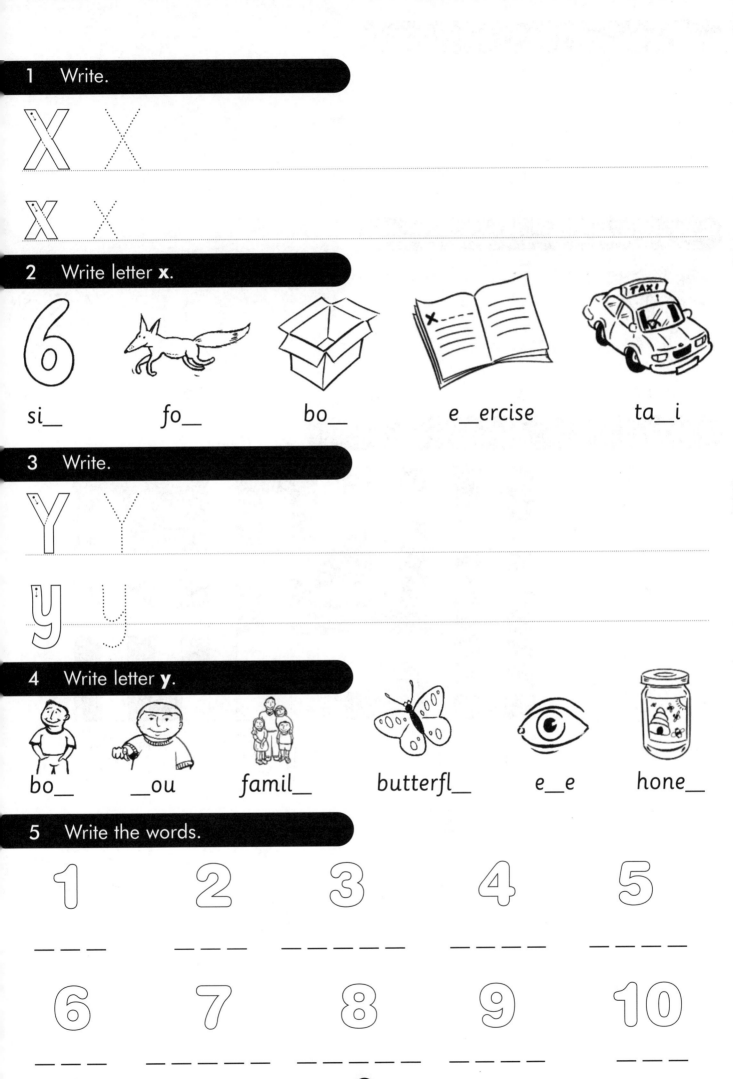

si__   fo__   bo__   e__ercise   ta__i

3 Write.

Y Y Y

y y y

4 Write letter **y**.

bo__   __ou   famil__   butterfl__   e__e   hone__

5 Write the words.

1   2   3   4   5

_ _ _   _ _ _   _ _ _ _   _ _ _ _   _ _ _ _

6   7   8   9   10

_ _ _   _ _ _ _   _ _ _ _ _   _ _ _ _   _ _ _

1 Write.

z z

z z

2 Write letter **z**.

   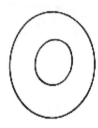 

_ebra   _oo   _ig_ag   _ero   pi_ _a

3 Look at the pictures and write the words.

6

9

10

13

14

15

1

2

3

4

5

7

8

11

12

16